NOTES FROM 1619

A Poetic 400-Year Reflection

Horace Mungin

EVENING POST BOOKS
Our Accent Is Southern!

Mungin, Horace. Notes from 1619: A Poetic 400-Year Reflection.
Published by Evening Post Books, Charleston, South Carolina.

ISBN-13: 978-1-929647-51-4

Cover and interior design by Michael J. Nolan

Contents

Acknowledgments

I love libraries and I love librarians. Here is the reason why: the first elementary school I attended was P.S. 89 in Harlem. The school was across the street from the 135th Street Branch of the New York City Public Library. My school partnered with the library in an after-school program called Story Hour. After school, the children were escorted across the street to the library to participate in the Story Hour program. We sat in little chairs and on the floor in a semicircle around pretty librarians who read wonderful stories of enchantment, discovery, and adventure to us.

More than 70 years later, I still have an image of one of those librarians in my mind's eye. She wore a blue suit and a white, ruffled blouse. She had jet black wavy hair that looked like she went to the hairdresser every day. Her face was bright and her eyes sparkled through black-framed glasses and always seemed to be singling me out from the others. She exuded a form of dignity I was seldom exposed to in the other circumstances of my life. When she read, the words seemed to form on her lips so that I could see and touch them. Her voice must have been angelic because I never heard it. As she read, my eyes grabbed the words from her lips and I was engulfed in their meanings.

I don't remember her name — I may have never known it, but her image and her gentleness are a part of me. There was something special going on between me and those black librarians. Story Hour was a five-days-a-week program and I never missed a session, I loved it so much. I was learning that I could experience the world through the pages of a book. This was the experience that planted a literary seed in me. As I became better at reading, I would check out books from the public library, five at a time. I never felt prouder than those days I walked home with an arm full of library books. I give thankful acknowledgment to those librarians and to that library for planting in me the idea that I could write. This is why I love libraries and this is why I love librarians.

I will also acknowledge the resiliency of my people who, over the past 400 years, suffered the cruelty of enslavement, Jim Crow, and continuing deceptions, and still, through it all, contributed the labor that built America, and under the cruelest conditions imaginable produced a culture in America emulated and celebrated worldwide. I acknowledge the resiliency of African Americans as the source of my literary focus — I am made of the miracle that is these people.

I warmly acknowledge the mystic William Baldwin, whose love of nature makes me think of him as a modern day Henry David Thoreau, for shining a light in my path that directed me to the people who helped make this book a reality and for his wonderful words about this work.

Aïda Rogers and I first met at the 2005 South Carolina Book Fair in Columbia. Our lives crossed paths next when, in 2013, she invited me to contribute an essay for her anthology of South Carolina writers, *State of the Heart.* She is one of the people Baldwin pointed to when he learned that I was looking for an editor. I send an embracing acknowldgement to Aïda for editing and copyreading this work. Her speedy competence makes me long for a lasting literary alliance between us.

Marjory Wentworth, South Carolina's longest-serving poet laureate (2003–present) save for Archibald Hamilton Rutledge (1934–1973), is acknowledged here for writing the foreword to *Notes from 1619.* I take pride in the fact that this busy artist and scholar made time between all her many obligations to read my manuscript and praise it. She is an asset to her students, a credit to South Carolina's literary community, and a state treasure.

I thank Professor Damon L. Fordham for reading and contributing a cover endorsement to this book. For nearly three decades now, Brother Fordham has been a voice of reason in the Lowcountry. He is a *look before you leap* practitioner of logic and wisdom whose knowledge of history is extensive; he is an old soul.

Finally, I would like to thank and acknowledge John M. Burbage and Michael Nolan, publisher and executive editor at Evening Post Books, for publishing this volume of poetry. We believe *Notes from 1619* will stir excitement among all stripes of readers and prove it justifies our faith in this work.

Foreword

Silence is the enemy of history, and history is all we have.

The Coming, by Daniel Black

Horace Mungin's brave attempt to fight against the multiple manifestations of injustice imposed by the conscious erasure of African-American history is in keeping with the best of contemporary African-American literature. Like Daniel Black in his poetic and powerful novel *The Coming*, which deftly imagines the horrors of the Middle Passage, Mungin takes us back to the Cape Coast of Africa and tells the story of Khadija, "born to a time of trouble," who was captured, imprisoned and carried on the slave ship, *Clotilda* "to look upon the world/ That dark day of the/Darkest days in America." And so it begins, the narrative journey that sweeps through these poems describing the African experience in America, "in this vacuum where there is no God." Echoing Langston Hughes's famous poem "Let America Be America Again," Mungin lays it all out for us in his pivotal "America": "Let's start at the beginning — America/Has never been America...It was a mirage from the very/Beginning — maybe even a deception, a hoax/A myth and an elegantly grand dishonesty." From the "hocus-pocus" of the ways in which the Constitution did not apply to black people, to the failures of Reconstruction and all that follows, Mungin weaves our history together until the present day and the election of Donald Trump to the presidency, when white voters "risked the narrow/Sliver of decency that keeps the country from sinking." This is a narrative we've never heard told in quite this way, and it provides a context and an understanding long missing from our national conversation.

Mungin has done his research, and in doing so he has found anecdotes that embody lived African-American experience, from slavery and the lynchings that characterized the Jim Crow period, through present-day murders of unarmed black men by police officers. In *Notes from 1619, A Poetic 400-Year Reflection*, Mungin holds up a mirror to the past. He never blinks or dodges the truth. Speaking truth to power in each poem, Mungin tells us stories that are left out of the history books. These are necessary stories, the ones we need to keep telling in order to heal and become the America we can only dream of, a place where "the triumph of Our Nourished/Notion of Freedom" can flourish and blossom.

After "Jim Crow" the poems are more self-reflective, but this one is like a bridge between past and present. Almost every line begins with the phrase "Jim Crow," followed by the listing of places Jim Crow "flourished" — from schools to hospitals in the United States until today. The final couplet comes down like a hammer: "Jim Crow Jim Crow/Jim Crowed to the end."

Despite these despairing lines, there are moments of light scattered like stars throughout this book. Mungin celebrates musicians Charlie Parker and Billie Holiday, and artist Hampton Olfus; revolutionary book dealer Una Mulzac and poet Amiri Baraka. Poems about Mungin's family members remind us of the glory of lives richly lived in the face of racism. That's the wonder of it all. And the honesty that characterizes the early poems in this collection is carried through to the end with tough poems about losing his beloved brother and battling cancer. Like all great poets, Mungin reaches a profound understanding about the mystery behind the inexplicable. In a moving poem about making peace with a father who was often violent and drunk, Mungin begins by saying: "I like to think that I turned out to/Be the person my father would/Have wanted himself to be ..." Here, the poet acknowledges the circumstances that prevented his father from living the life he could have lived and being the man he could have been in a country without racism, and in doing so Mungin makes peace with the demons of the past while acknowledging his good fortune at being born later. Therein lies the hope Mungin shares with all of us. "The more I look at a thing/The clearer it becomes to me..." Whether he is talking about his own life or the state of America, Mungin shares his wisdom and clarity in the poems in *Notes from 1619*.

Marjory Wentworth, South Carolina Poet Laureate

Author's Note

Notes from 1619 is a collection of poetry written in commemoration of one man's ancestral linkage to the arrival of the first Africans 400 years ago in what was to become the United States of America. It is a testimony on the intervening events that have shaped and propelled black lives since Jamestown, and in that sense it represents the stories of the current 40 million African Americans who are the descendants of an enslaved people — making *Notes from 1619* their narrative, too.

The mixture of poems is organized in a chronology that mirrors the distressing history of race relations in America. The journey starts with a voyeur's view of the celebratory dance of a naked young bride-to-be engaging alone in her tribal fertility pirouette — a beach scene that conveys a sense of the tranquil paradise that existed before the arrival of the barbarians. The next poem explodes into a scene of carnage, fire, pillage, and rampage as humans are forcibly loaded into ships for the Middle Passage, and from there the poems quickly assemble to recount the story of race in America.

One reader of the manuscript asked me if I thought all white people were racist. I was momentarily dazed because my immediate reaction was that this question was asked because that is the impression this reader arrived at from reading my poems. I quickly assured the reader that this was not the case. I even smiled and said that John Brown was one of my heroes. Upon further reflection, however, I realized that because the poems exposed white barbarism in the stark terms in which they were rendered, the reader had mistaken the bluntness of my poems for the blinding bitterness that would lead to the assertion that all whites are racist. So my answer to that reader should have been that I don't think that all white people are racist, but they all benefitted from racism, thus they all must contribute to the solution — that is the point of my edgy poems. So before you read on, let me assure you that I know that there are many, many unbiased white people who are self-assured enough that they feel that they would fare well in an unbiased society. They are the hope of this book.

There are poems that make visits to the treatment of the enslaved plantation population as well as poems that decry the hundred years of Jim Crow decrees that crippled African-American progress, and poems that point to the general hypocrisy of racism. The murderous period known as the Red Summer of 1919 unfolds in a poem that reads like scenes from a stage play. Just as it happened in history, the advent of the civil rights movement follows; then a little past halfway through the book, the poems pay tribute to people who mentored my interest in literary activism: poet Amiri Baraka and revolutionary book merchant Una Mulzac; and people who extolled African-American culture, Charlie Parker and Billie Holiday.

There are poems that measure the distance African Americans have travel from 1619 by exploring twentieth-century America in verses that use my immediate family as a microcosm for the larger African-American community. And I drop in a few poems on American politics like highway pileups that the reader will rubberneck by before realizing that, through the fears of demographic upheaval, all American politics is linked to 1619.

Reading *Notes from 1619* is not meant to be a sunny stroll in the park, but rather a trek through a minefield that makes you better for having successfully maneuvered through it. Reading *Notes from 1619* is, perhaps, the closest many of you will ever get to the pain created by white supremacy and suffered by African Americans and, it is my hope, move you to become a catalyst for justice now.

Last Dance of the Forest Virgin

Fatimah emerged from the high forest foliage
To the desolate ocean shore wrapped in indigo
Her delicate naked feet covering a million
Grains of hot white sand with each dancing step
Her dark body glistening from the yellow rays
Of a natural sun that nevertheless paid her tribute
Her breasts like protruding pyramids tilted skywards
As she twirled on sobering thighs her thin long arms
Held up in praise of Jah on this her wedding day

This is her tribal ceremonial custom a solitary
Baptism in sun and sand naked and unrestrained
Seeking universal blessings for a fertile matrimony
Through a dance stimulating abundant fruitfulness

Ocean waves applauded approvingly upon the shore
Birds chirped an exuberant nuptial harmony
All of the elements of nature showered favorably
As Fatimah bowed gracefully three times her arms
Stretched out in humble offerings like a Goddess.

Ras the Exhorter

Listen brothers and sisters
To the mournful cry of a people
Being led to the dock of defeat and despair
Herded onto the ships of bondage
While the past severed in a night
Red of fire
And the fortunate died
Clinging to the bosom of Mother Africa
And upon the blooded shore
Laid a child drowned
While in search of its mother
Who at that very instant
(Upon a vessel destined for America)
Sang…the first song of terror
The first song of sorrow
The first song of shame and survival
The first Blues

Listen brothers and sisters
To the spirit of that child
As it whispers in the wind
The rumors of rebellion
To an African who had not yet lost himself
And who upon hearing these rumors
Died in mutiny
And the many passively buried him
Deafened by the sound of
Whispered rumors in the wind
A people withered in the fields
For a second and a third century
But only those who heard the whispered
Rumors of a child in search
Lived a death of defiance

Brothers and sisters
A child has not seen its mother
For three hundred years and
Longs to hold her near
And still he whispers
In the wind the rumors of liberation
And when we too hear
The whispered rumors in the wind
The search of a child shall be over.

KHADIJA

Khadija was born in a village on the high
Grassy mountains of the Wolof people
All her years she was a radiant flower
When Khadija was eighteen she
Stood under the nuptial canopy

On the morning of her nineteenth birthday
Khadija took a walk amid the tribal safe
Savannahs to celebrate her induction
Into motherhood for some time during
Her year of marriage to Joseph to
Procreate a little Bird flew into her nest

Lurking unseen in the high savannahs
A marauding horde of human traders
Abducted Khadija and her bird then
In exchange for whiskey they turned
Them over to pale stringy-haired barbarians

Khadija was chained to a crew of
Other wretches and force-marched
Over several nights and days two
Hundred miles to the Gorée Island
To the Cape Coast Castle in preparation
For an upper deck spot on the *Clotilda*
In 1859 the concluding vessel of evil
The last slave ship to the United States.

The voyage was long and torturous
The sun was hot, the gruel was thin
Each day Khadija silently called out
Joseph's name and she named the
Growing bird nestled in her nest
Kuzaliwa kwa wakati wa shida
(born to a time of trouble)

The slave ship *Clotilda* cut through the waves
All around there was but blue skies and seas

They were engulfed in a world of indigo
One evening the woman chained next to Khadija
Whose markings suggest she was a princess
Broke loose and threw her body over the
Railing into the depths of the ocean below

Khadija was mesmerized by this action
Causing thoughts of her own pending destiny
She dreamt of Joseph's bewilderment
And the uncertain fate of her caught bird
The thought that her bird might appear
Before this nightmare ended tormented her

Khadija looked for a chance to join the
Emancipated princess on the ocean floor
And though her leg irons were fastened
Secure to the pinched she was resolute
That the ocean was where she would leap

The days and the weeks mounted with
The misery as the bird now moved often
Then early in the haze of a morning hue
Off in a far corner of the indigo globe
Appeared a gray mass growing larger
And clearer as the *Clotilda* advanced

It was halfway through the night when
The ship came to a halt and now only
Swayed with the motion of the ocean
Anxiety arose for Khadija and the others
As they were dragged, pulled and carried
Down the gangway, their legs in rebellion

Kuzaliwa kwa wakati wa shida
(born to a time of trouble)
Came out to look upon the world
That dark day of the
Darkest days in America.

The Lashing of Patsey of Bayou Boeuf Plantation

Patsey was a demure charming young woman of
Twenty-three but she also possessed a regal aura
And a majestic stature and she was a slave on the
Plantation of Edwin Epps of Bayou Boeuf on the Red River
She was enchanting, far more than Mistress Epps
Or any white woman in Louisiana to her master

Edwin Epps, brutal and mean, with lust and power lay
Patsey to his pleasure in a most foul way not once
Many times she cut off all feelings; all emotions
And lay there a mere receptacle for his lewd desire
He danced the dance of a broken man making
Mistress Epps the third leg to this unbalanced stool

To this Mistress Epps did not take lightly but
Directed her bile at Patsey, not her devil husband
By now so bewitched by his lust for Patsey he
Was willing to rid his presence of his infuriating wife
Who so hated and envied Patsey she tormented her
Often each chance that came with words and violence
Rationed her no soap with which to bathe Epps's scent away

One day to a nearby plantation Patsey did stray
For a piece of soap from a kindly soul and found
Missing from her place in the field Epps flew into a
Jealous rage, on her return accused her absence on
A vile craving and not the want for soap which she
Produced in hand saying how mistress does not give
Her a ration as she does with all the others

Now Epps blinded by fury and a thirst for blood
Coaxed on by his mistress's presence; she watched
From the big-house veranda her children at her side
And the slaves threw aside their chores for the moment
A spectacle of epic proportions drew them to disregard
Whatever the consequences should be to witness what's
Possible in this vacuum where there is no God — no God

Platt stood near Patsey; between her and Epps could he
Protect her just this once more and his eyes soften to plead
Her case, but Epps, devil of a man as he is took his foot
And marked in the sand the four spots he wanted stakes
To be driven into the ground and ordered that Patsey be
Stripped of every article of clothes then had this poor
Naked girl tied face down to the earth he handed Platt
A sturdy lash then ordered Platt in this vacuum where
There is no God to whip the skin from off her hide.

Platt sent to her back some moderate licks which
Incensed Epps and his mistress all the more
Give it to her with all you've got or you will feel it next
Epps threatened grieving Platt beseeching God to appear
Platt held his lash still hoping this fulfilled his master's will
But the devil pined for more; Platt laid out ten more licks
And threw the whip to the ground and his life on the line

Then this monster could not get his fill picked up the lash
And whipped her still she moaned and pleaded and prayed
That God would seal the vacuum where hate resided, her
Back a bloodied mess as the whip tore out her flesh
Epps noticed the result he could not get from her the
Times he thrust his pelvis to her groin in his mind now
How she groaned as he struck again and again his mistress saw
In his eyes the pleasure he imagined between Patsey's thighs

Finally it was over and Patsey unconscious removed
To the slave quarters to be nursed and prayed over
That she might die and be relieved of the curse of
Edwin Epps and Mistress Epps of the Bayou Boeuf
Plantation — but if she lived it be God's will.

The Red Summer of 1919

June:
It was a warm Saturday morning
The feel of the air and the bright
Sun in the sky warned everyone
To get strenuous chores done early
To avoid the scorching later-day heat
Ruth Dunlop took Sunday's apple pie
Out of the oven before ten Saturday
Morning Mr. Dunlop had mended the
South gate fence that kept his nine
Jersey cows from roaming off

All over the county people scurried
To beat the heat, but there was another
Event that impelled the entire region
To have free time by early evening
While God wondered how a whole
Community of people could contemplate
Such a grim deed absent a moral tinge

Slim Smithers loaded his Kodak
Duaflex camera and put three extra rolls
Of photo film in his cloth carry sack
He had a hundred thick 3 x 5 paper
Postcard sheets to print his pictures
Portraying a uniquely American evil

Albert Alston and his son Richard
Loaded his horse-drawn lunch wagon
With bags of roasted peanuts, Life Savers
And Pep-O-Mints and individually
Wrapped chocolate Tasty Cakes and
A barrel of Dr. Pepper covered with
Large chunks of chipped ice to sell
Like at the glittery County Fair

The three Biltmore cousins went down
To the swimming hole that morning
But kept a sharp eye on the movement
Of the sun, they knew that when
The sun was to the right side of
The twin oak trees dividing the dirt
Road back into town it was time
For them to head home if they
Wanted to witness the spectacle

Sheriff Gilroy had gone over the plan
With an ad hoc committee of the town's
Men who he was sure would be on time
The condemned man paced anxiously
And prayed hopelessly in a secured cell

Sheriff Gilroy sat his feet up on the desk
Killing time and whistling Dixie

There was a somber air of excitement
In all of Belton County foreshadowing
The gathering in the town of Pine Bluff
Wives and husbands packed a lunch for
Themselves and their children who were
Keen to absorb this tradition for their
Generation to institutionalize and pass on

The morning newspapers described the event
In thorough detail; date, time, offense
And even an account and comparison
Of the last such event in the county
The evening newspaper assigned
One reporter and two photographers
The whole affair emanated an aura of
Righteous cohesive tribal patriotism

All of white Pine Bluff knew the hour
To assemble in the rear of the jail
Was when the clock strikes four
Right across the street from the
First Missionary Church of God in Christ
There is a sturdy tree there with high
Substantial limbs and an active history

July:
When World War One began African-American
Men viewed the conflict as an opportunity
To prove their loyalty, patriotism, and worthiness
For equal treatment in the United States
They wanted to fight to earn the respect of
White citizens and the white government
African-American men eagerly joined the
Four existing regiments of all-black troops
They didn't wait to be selected by the new
Draft system — they joined voluntarily
But in the South it was fairly common
For Southern postal workers to deliberately
Withhold the draft registration notices of
Eligible black men and have them arrested
For being draft dodgers

Racist white officers sabotaged the reputations
Of African-American military units; they were
Treated with extreme hostility and sometimes
Went for long periods without proper clothing
And were often given the most degrading chores at
Home and the most dangerous ones in combat

White combat units didn't perform well when
Fighting alongside black units endangering
Many missions and the war itself
Because the French used colonial troops
From Senegal, they had experience in deploying

Black soldiers in combat so the U.S. assigned
The black 93rd Infantry Division to France, the first
African-American combat troops to set foot
On French soil was the 369th Infantry

After three weeks the regiment was sent
To the front lines in a region just west of
The Argonne Forest; for nearly a month
They held their position against German assaults
Proving their tenacity once again by helping
The French drive the Germans from their
Trenches during an important counteroffensive
Proudly earning the nickname Harlem Hellfighters

The history of the Harlem Hell-ighters belonged to
Sargeant Willie Brown of Charleston, South Carolina
He earned it through hardship and suffering
He was a Harlem Hellfighter deserving admiration
He was home in Charleston this July on leave before
He was to report to Fort Hood, Texas to receive his
Honorable discharge and now strolling King Street
With his fiancée Rebecca Quail in uniform seeking
The respectful recognition he fought in the war to earn

They were approached by a gang of white men
Who first blocked their passageway forcing
Them into the street, then the gang circled
The couple screaming at Willie Brown to
Take off the uniform of their country
Knocking off his hat and laughing at what
They called a monkey in uniform

Then they tightened the circle grabbing Rebecca
By her arm Willie fearing the danger struck back
And the scuffle commenced until the police arrived
To arrest both Willie and Rebecca
And took them off to jail

In an hour Rebecca was released, Willie had been
Badly beaten and needed medical attention

He was retained in a jail cell in poor condition
The next morning Willie was found hanging
From a pipe in the ceiling, the city newspaper
Headlined the event in this manner:
Negro disgraced uniform in street brawl
Hangs self in jail cell

August:
Lewis Leland was a God-fearing Christian, a man
Of morals and high standards; a preacher man
Married to a woman of identical matching qualities
They had two teenage sons 15 and 13 and a daughter
Of eight, who were being brought up in the manner
Of their parents; poor, prideful and respectful of
Themselves and others black and white

The Lelands lived a nearly self-sufficient existence
They raised chickens, hogs and had two cows
And they planted a substantial vegetable garden
All of which they were very private about

Lewis Leland used his meager pastor's salary
To buy the few things his family needed and
He gave the balance to needy church families
He was a Bible-reading God-fearing man with
Next to no contact with white people in Clark
County, Mississippi

Many whites in the county had heard of the
Preacher Lewis Leland, he was for them
Out of sight, out of mind until the day the
Newly elected County Clerk sent a bogus
Delinquent property tax notice by messenger
To the Leland household and other black
Clark County citizens

As other black citizens sold off livestock
And devised other means of meeting the
Demands of the swindle, Lewis Leland
Ignored the bill refusing to recognize it
As legitimate, made up in his mind that
He would never pay it

The newly elected County Clerk took
Lewis Leland's noncompliance as a personal
Affront and a hindrance to him carrying out
The duties of his office even though the tax
Was part of his scheme to confiscate Negro
Land to sell to whites at rates that would
Increase white property ownership

The clerk spied on Lewis Leland by probing
Other Negroes about any of his affairs
One told him that the preacher had prayed
For the right to vote another said that
The preacher hated evil which the clerk
Interpreted as meaning white, yet another
Negro described the Leland family as uppity

The County Clerk retold the Leland story
In seditious terms to the county's white
Citizens; made it sound like the Leland family
Was engaging in treason and he offered as
Evidence the altered words of three Negroes
And the unpaid tax invoice

This lie mixed among the county's white
Population growing uglier in each telling until
The idea to take corrective action was born
No Negro family in Clark County should be
Permitted to challenge white tradition and
Survive to spread sedition to other Negroes
And pretty soon the whole county would be
Going to hell in a handbasket

It didn't take long maybe a week or two
For the rumors to take hold and drive
White citizens stark raving mad to put
These uppity Negroes in their place and
Make an example for all the Negroes of
Clark County to fear

A plan soon developed amongst that group of
Clark County men who saw it as their duty
To regulate and dispense Negro discipline
The plan was a hooded early morning ride
Out to the Leland property to round up the entire
Clan and wagon tote them to the Hanging Bridge

The Shubuta Bridge is a wooden truss bridge
That spans the Chickasawhay River
In Southeastern Mississippi known as the
Hanging Bridge where white Clark County citizens
Often lined up to watch the swinging bodies
Of unfortunate black souls

During the wagon ride to the bridge the
Leland family, all five, bounded hand and
Foot looked through brave eyes giving
Courage to each other, only the father spoke these
Words: Don't you worry my dear ones
Nary a white man, woman or child of a past
Present or future generation shall escape
The fires of hell for all eternity
They shall all burn in the inferno of hell
My God tells me so.

An Appeal to White People

They give you me to look down upon
My misery made you feel superior
So happily shielded from my wretchedness you
Never noticed that they are picking
Your pockets too/using you to buffer
Them from my retribution for their terror
Wake up white people

They put you at the front of the bus
Your own waiting room/a lunch counter
All your own/they send your children to
Better funded schools/let you work with skilled tools
Let you vote for their lackeys who regulate
Your existence and mind/
Wake up white people

Right now their economic noose is tightened
Round your neck and mine
There is no longer even a farce of a livable wage
They give our jobs to foreigners and robots
With artificial intelligence/artificial intelligence
Wake up white people

Before long it will be too late
The big white boss man will be gone
And close the gate/you too will be left behind
Fighting for scraps off the rich's plates
Unite with me/let's set things straight
Wake up white people

Crumble Wall Street a start
Dismantle their tangled web
Appeal to their sense of fair play
But hold a dagger to their heart
United to show our determination
To share in the wealth of this nation
Wake up white people.

A Little Black Boy

I'm just a little black boy
I like video games, hip hop music
Candy, chips and dips, Air Jordan s
Laughing out loud, walking free
I be
Trying to reach black adulthood in
America

I'm just a little black boy
Already cheated, prey for the system,
From a mistreated history, oh, how they fear me,
Snuff out my potentials to uplift my people
Stop and Frisk me, Bait and Switch me,
Prison pipeline me, disenfranchise me
All to stop me, now you see me
Trying to reach black adulthood in
America

I'm just a little black boy
Been told to be careful/the talk
Black boys get from black parents on how
What I say to white policemen should
Be measured in servile drabness always
Keeping my hands where they see them
Empty
Then pray that this is not the vacant-eyed one
In every five that I may live another day
Trying to reach black adulthood in
America.

The Lie of a Hundred Generations

First they manufactured the supreme lie
An enabling lie, an empowering lie –
A sanctioning lie — a gargantuan lie
They gave the lie the veneer of having
Been mandated from the Creator
Of heaven and earth, of wind and sea
Of man and mankind and therefore
An authorizing lie dehumanizing me
And my kind

They came out of Africa
With treasured commodities of gum, ivory, gold
Rice, camwood, beeswax, and humans
To turn into slaves, all to create
The Atlantic Consumer Culture
They laid the lie out like a blanket of their
Evil and praised the Creator for its Creation

American goods were in demand in Sierra Leone
British goods were in demand in Philadelphia
And African labor was in demand everywhere
They lied that my kind was lower than human
Of another species nearer to ape than to human
This lie made possible the sadistic treatment
Of humans by mutant humans only in existence
Themselves since the short time distance after
The last Ice Age and they came stumbling from
The caves of Europe to subjugate the world

This lie removed the taint from the lash
This lie allowed ruthlessness to portray itself
As a socially enriching advancement
This lie built fortunes that gave high
Perch to moral monsters

A war between countrymen was fought
Over the lie or how it had dehumanized the liars
And brutalized and dehumanized the lied about

The liars lost the war but were allowed to reshape
And codify the lie into rules and regulations
Enshrine into laws and the anguish of the South
Empower Jim Crow generations with white privileges

The civil rights movement took to the streets
And brutal rural country roads against the lie
And the warnings of moving too quickly
With signs that proclaimed
I Am A Man
Meaning that me and my kind are indeed humans
And for you to become human too
You have to un-tell the lie
To claim your own humanity
By recognizing me as your equal

The lie has survived into modern times
To impeach your noble notions of yourselves
As a people content with God and a wobbled
Experiment with freedom and democracy
That lost its moral base in your refusal to
See me and my kind as humans and reject
The reality that black lives matter — too

When comes your generation that un-tell the lie
Un-tell the lie, un-tell the lie, un-tell the lie
Un-tell the lie, un-tell the lie, un-tell the lie
Un-tell the lie, un-tell the lie, un-tell the lie
Un-tell the lie, un-tell the lie, un-tell the lie
For it will be on what you do and not do
That your story shall hang.

The Water Fountain

I know that you wouldn't want me to bring this up
And I wonder why that is, could it be your shame,
Your vanity, your regret, or your guilt
When you are made to remember these circumstances
You lay the blame down to another generation
To assign culpability on your ancestors
You disown their evil exploits without disowning them
Or that you spring from them as inheritor of the privileges
Their enforced supremacy created for them and for you

Nor do you like me to mention that it took federal laws to
Cease the practice of your advantages through oppression

Because I know that there is nothing but law;
Not your morality or your religion, nor your benevolence
Which could prevent you from resuming the practice and
Revive all the social, cultural, and economic amenities
That accompanies White Only water fountains
Once your needs arise, I stand watch over
Water fountains as the first sign of recidivism.

Legacy
(for Fannie Lou Hamer)

Born just a short distance from bondage time
Into a life of servitude, deprivation, and bigotry
The daughter of a sharecropper
The wife of a sharecropper
The Life of a Sharecropper
There appeared no way out
This was all there was going to be
Not even the faintest glimmer of hope

Born with God's gift of courage and a sense
Of self that would not be subjugated by any other
She was a human woman being who
One day discovered the vote and the power it held
For this she was banned from her hut on the plantation
And into a life of gallantry where her gospel singing
Stiffened backs and inspired resolve in a cowered people

They sent her from her home, they threatened her
They shot at her, they followed her around
They beat her near blind — like she was a man
Her mission and her song came from on high
Such enduring courage they had never encountered
As with this woman who came to right ancient wrongs
And would not be denied the vote for us all

She made her mark testifying at the Democratic
National Convention in New Jersey, in 1964
She became a national spearhead to win the vote
Her leadership abilities organized people to a cause
She built consequential institutions that helped
Bring dignity, power, hope, and the vote to us all
Her remains in Ruleville, Mississippi, her spirit roams the
Nation, her soul rests in eternity, her name is
Fannie Lou Hamer.

America

Let's start at the beginning — America
Has never been America
The landowners wrote some noble words on
Sheets of paper as the guide for the nation's
Behavior, but neither they nor their descendants
Have been able to reproduce the nobility of those
Sentiments expressed on paper in their legislatures
In their towns, in their cities, on their streets
In their homes, schools, churches, indeed,
Not even in their hearts

It was a mirage from the very
Beginning — maybe even a deception, a hoax
A myth and an elegantly grand dishonesty — for
What happened to the indigenous people who
Lived here and the kidnapped African people
Brought here in chains was not congruent
With the noble words on those sheets of paper

A deliriously schizophrenic nation traveled
Through the centuries glorifying the words,
Exalting the words, believing in the words, bragging
Of a nation above all other nations, originated
By the agitation of its land-owning Founding Fathers
Although the contradictions they lived, produced
Carnage to all but the landowners and their tribe
And then there did come a time when their tribe was
Led into carnage because the landowners divided into
A North/South dispute over the continuance of slavery

The robber barons gobbled up control of all
Wealth-producing processes and proportioned
A society of vacillating economic levels and
Social privileges contingent on tribal membership
Over whom they became the all-powerful oligarchy

The oligarchy divided the riches of the nation
Amongst a tiny one percent of the population; the banks
The railroads, the oil fields, the shipping lanes, the stock market
Then later, the automobiles, the airways, and manufacturing
And they produced a white ruling class to oversee their
Kingdom and a white managing class to select
Who eats and to whom privilege is administered
All this was done under the guise of those
Noble words written in a document known as
The Constitution of the United States of America
Bringing honor and privileges to members, but
Why the noble words remained only an aspiration
To all else is explained with sleight of hand,
Hocus-pocus and unfulfilled promises of a better future

Even after the monumental failures of Reconstruction and the
Rise of the Ku Klux Klan the United States restored
Control of the South to white supremacists, the Negro was
Disfranchised and betrayed by his country, even after
Negroes enlisted or were drafted into two world wars
To preserve the sacredness of those noble words
In the hopes of making them true for themselves
The oligarchy ordered the ruling class to warn Negroes
Against moving too fast towards freedom — cautioning them of
Their aspirations for freedom; even after 1919's Red Summer
Of lynching they scolded Negroes for wanting too much freedom
Even after Emmett Till was murdered they bellowed — too much, too soon
About the dissent and the ruling class whites passed the edict down
To the managing class whites to stifle all black attempts to bridge the gaps

One woman's refusal to give up her seat on a bus cracked
Open the lid on centuries' long bottled-up angry black frustration
And erupted into a nationwide movement for black freedom
The nonviolent civil rights era came to be after the
Montgomery bus boycott in 1955 that briefly elevated names like
Jo Ann Robinson, Claudette Colvin, and Mary Louise Smith

With the spilling of blood came other victories; the Civil Rights
Act, the Voting Rights Act, the Equal Employment Opportunity
Commission, America seemed to be growing a conscience
Just at the time when African Americans were awakening to the lie
And beginning to disbelieve what had been said about them by
White people, they were awakening to a history of themselves
That gave them racial pride, racial confidence and a racial identity

A few black men came to the notion that the problem was not of
A black construction or of a black import, or black ownership
The problem, these handful discovered, was solely because they were black
The country they lived in was constructed entirely for the security of
White people — read the Constitution — which considered them three-fifths of
A person in a compromise that proportioned more legislative seats for the
Slaveholding Southern states — three-fifths of a person from 1787 until 1865
Else they would have been slaughtered and disregarded like the native people
So the problem does not belong to the African-American people

The problem persists because present-day white people don't
Want to confront the wickedness of their ancestors, or the
Auction block, or the compromise or the chains, or the whip or the lash
Or the limbs pulled apart, or the raped girl or the child sold off, or the
Young man tied all day to a tree in the sun or the wife sold down
The river or mass lynching, or the fury of a white lynch mob
Or a hundred years of Jim Crow, or the depths of the evil from which
They spring — there is the problem; one of the white world's construction

For them to dredge up this evil would be to accept their association
With it and validate their kinship with those who invented this evil
To remember this wickedness would require them to wear the cloak
Of inhumanity and offer an apology — and to surrender a restoration to
The survivors of the evil; a burden so revolting no white person can
Endure it, so they deny the reality, they would much prefer to
Remain ignorant of it — What's really needed here James Baldwin once
Said, is: White History Week — the white man needs to understand
All of his history — needs to be pinned to it, gathered and penetrable
Otherwise here is what happens

White Evangelicals abandoned God's morality and all
The ethics they pretend to know from the Bible to support
A decadent man whose wicked moral excesses of
Twenty-five years are well documented in print,
On audio tapes, in videos, from his own admission
White American voters in the biggest departure of
Moral judgment since slavery risked the narrow
Sliver of decency that keeps the country from sinking
Altogether to support this man whose marketing promise
Is that he will make America great again negating the
Necessity to dredge up old history — in his world, it didn't happen
He will erect a wall to create a reality so white the noble
Words of the Founding Fathers will ring true again.

Jim Crow

Jim Crow where truth can't go
Jim Crow where freedom can't fly
Jim Crow where light can't shine
Jim Crow where Justice is denied

Jim Crow was born in the South
Jim Crow was raised in the West
Jim Crow was schooled in the East
Jim Crow worked in the North
Jim Crow flourished in
The United States of America
Restricting black lives and progress
For a hundred years

Jim Crow in schools
Jim Crow in jails
Jim Crow in banks
Jim Crow in hospitals
Jim Crow in the workplace
Jim Crow in public transportation
Jim Crow at the lunch counters
Jim Crow justice
Jim Crow water fountains
Jim Crow housing
Jim Crow text books
Jim Crow preachers
Jim Crow teachers
Jim Crow judges
Jim Crow police

Jim Crow Reconstruction
Jim Crow Birth of a Nation
Jim Crow white lynch mob
Jim Crow poll taxes
Jim Crow separate but equal

Jim Crow miscegenation
Jim Crow Bible
Jim Crow stifling
Jim Crow white knight of the Ku Klux Klan

Then came the civil rights movement
Chipping away at Jim Crow
Chiseled it down to Jim Crow lite
Jim Crow weakened and a black
President was elected
Creating the inevitable white backlash
In 2016 down on its dying bed
Jim Crow heaved a despe rate reprieve
To puke out the four-year campaign
Called Make America Great Again

Jim Crow, Jim Crow
Jim Crowed to the end.

The Third Eye

I look through my eyes as a man
I see abundant possibilities
I look through my eyes as an American
I am overwhelmed by the alluring but unfulfilled opportunities
I look through my eyes as an African-American man
And I see the possibilities and the opportunities
Of my other eyes crumble before my eyes
I have three eyes.

Police Oppression

The weight of police oppression
Is so crushingly debilitating
My breath exhausts, my mind scrambles,
My spirit falls

And then to see the system fail
All powers shore up the wrong
And spite again that black boy

To tell all like him what they can expect
From a white country
Where might makes right

To turn it around
We may have to
Go underground.

Our Nourished Notion of Freedom

We nourished a notion of freedom
A notion of liberty and unfettered
Membership in the American family
We nourished a notion of equality and love
Brotherhood and camaraderie where not
Only our contributions are valued but
We too are embraced and welcomed.

We suffered the ocean and the chains
And the auction block, we suffered
The whip and the lash and our families torn out
We planted the fields, harvested the crops,
Cultivated the rice and picked the cotton
That made America rich and our work
Made white privilege possible and enduring.

We nourished the notion long
And slowly pulled it forward
We hauled it onward amidst
All of your opposition: hooded
Terrorizing, deceit, fraudulence
Trickery, bile and hocus-pocus
We gently towed our nourished
Notion century by century, hope
Faith, generation by generation
One by one by one, step by step
And now the time has truly come.

Our nourished notion blossoms as
You shed your excessive scorn
America cannot be America without
The triumph of Our Nourished
Notion of Freedom.

On the Road to Impeachment

America is a noble idea reaching
Toward its third century
A country of free people
Ruled by laws and principles
Guided by a constitution
That regulates and separates
The powers of the three
Major dominions of government

This system held for hundreds
Of years while America inched
Slowly towards the concept of
An equitable and inclusive society
Even for those abused in America's
Original sin; each leap forward
Created a lurch backwards impairing
Progress but unable to forever stall it

The lawful grounds equality gained
Came most with the existence of
The civil rights movement while
The Black Arts Movement boosts
Acceptance of culture, traditions
History and prideful differences

Then the time arrived when the future
Racial demographic could be extrapolated
With the largest group losing power
The specter unnerved the majority
Desperate to reverse or delay the
Inevitable coming fate they whined
That a savior from anywhere would do

He would have to be unscrupulous
Media savvy and a top weaver of lies
He would have to be ever shameless
And shameful simultaneously
He would have to be a transactional

Human without a spirit or a heart
He would have to wear the cloak
Of inhumanity unabashed by reality

This demon was found in the person
Of a real estate wheeler-dealer from
The place the rest of the country hated
Most; New York City, New York City
Where the demon had developed and
Perfected the high art of the swindle

The voters hired this demon to show
The real politicians how disappointed
They were with being deceived year
After year; they wanted this demon to
Upset the apple cart so that regular
Politicians' lessons learned, would slow
The demographic shift and put things
Back together right this time

But the demon took the power to his head
Disregarded all the protocols by breaching
All the tenets that held American structure
Together and worked to mediate disputes
This demon devastated the domestic
Intelligence and security service, degraded the
Quality of the administration cabinet members
He discredited the foreign intelligence service

He weakened the court system and rendered
The Congress powerless; a mere wordy
Toothless assemblage, all bark no bite
That allowed the demon to violate
Democratic norms free of charge now
Democracy is in the ICU and America is
Mortally wounded without any assurance
Of its survival except if it impeached.

Amiri Baraka

LeRoi Jones left Greenwich Village and the literary life of
White bohemia; a world of Kerouac, Burroughs, and Ginsberg
Malcolm X had been murdered to silence his voice and vision
The void was immediately gathering monumental setbacks

LeRoi Jones divested himself of his white life
A wife and daughter and his slave name
He arrived to Harlem Amiri Baraka, like a drum and spear
To create and guide the black consciousness movement
Malcolm X was fermenting in black American minds

Amiri Baraka founded the Black Arts Repertory Theatre
To explore new ways to present the black experience
Gathering Ed Bullins, Sun Ra, Larry Neal, the BAM
Coterie formed in Harlem and reached outwards

Like Charleston's in Harlem, like Atlanta's in Harlem
Like Chicago's in Harlem, like Watts's in Harlem
And Akron, Oakland, and South Philadelphia, Roxbury,
And Memphis, Houston, Charlotte, and Birmingham, they
Are all Harlem now because BAM led; they followed
The Black Arts Movement

The black consciousness movement joined together
Vast regions and a huge array of people to form a cultural
Union of remembrance of the past as they forged the road
To the future; a future born in celebration of the
Black Arts Movement of the 1960s

BAM, Baraka formed to fill the void that Malcolm left
BAM, Baraka said: One will learn God knows
What from God knows who

BAM brought change; somebody blew up old America.

Una Mulzac

If you don't know, learn, if you know, teach
Reads the sign hanging in the door of
The Liberation Bookstore on Lenox
Avenue in Harlem, New York City
During the latter years of the Black
Arts Movement

Created by a revolutionary sister the store
Known as the University on the Corner
Of Lenox Avenue (UCLA) nurtured
A generation to black cultural awareness

Una Mulzac phenomenon of a bloodline
That produced the first black commander of
A United States merchant marine ship
Her father, Hugh N. Mulzac, was ambitious

Una was born in Baltimore, raised in Brooklyn
Graduated from Girls High School
Worked at Random House
Encouraged scores of scholars from
Behind the counter of UCLA

She joined the revolution in Guyana
In the early 1960s and was severely
Injured by a bomb, she recovered
In the United States and returned to
The revolution until Guyana gained
Independence from Britain in 1966

She came back to New York City
To open the Liberation Bookstore
That became as storied as Lewis Michaux's
African National Memorial Bookstore
The House of Common Sense and the
Home of Proper Propaganda

Una protested war, racism, and police brutality
Every righteous battle was her battle, she
Was often arrested and called Mayor Giuliani
A fascist before it was plain to the rest of us

Cantankerous, Una had a running battle
With the city government; she was a
Revolutionary and a book dealer
Not a street sweeper — not that
She held anything against
Street sweepers, for her it was
A matter of knowing one's role.

Summer Frog's Mating Call

For hours during the last nights of spring
The baritone timbre of the pond summer
Frogs can be heard like a wave in the dark
Searching out for love, calling for a mate
A lover to enter the water to answer the call
Of the loudest, deepest, and longest timbre

Their planted webbed feet on long hind legs
Their forelegs with eager nuptial pads ready
To grip the moist wartless skin of a mate
Searching out the white throated sound
Of procreation
She lays a thousand eggs and he sprays
Them to his likeness
She moves on
And he sends out his call once more.

Poetry

What is Poetry?
Poetry is the poet's hammer and chisel,
Poetry is the poet's paint and brush,
Poetry is the poet's tool

What is Poetry?
Poetry is thought sprouting wings
Poetry is an idea shedding layers of its self
Poetry is the ballet words dance together

What is Poetry?
Poetry is that truth that survives the lie
Poetry is all we see in you and me
Poetry is the harmony of rhyme time

What is Poetry?
Poetry is different from the poet
Poetry is the poet's gatherings
Poetry is the temporary quenching of the poet's thirst

What is Poetry?
Poetry is that spot between hearing
And wondering
What it was you heard.

From 42 to 44

42 was a first for Major League Baseball
Some fans and some players reacted
With hatred, scorn, and death threats
Boos and ridicule met 42 at the plate
And on the field and in the locker room

42 stayed focused kept his eyes on the ball
And ran the bases unnerving the entire infield
Pitchers cracked whether 42 was at the plate
Or on base, he was going to steal a base or
Whack the ball out the park

The fans finally came around to cheer him
The players came to fear him
They all had to respect him
Though not as easy as it sounds
42 had cracked the color barrier in baseball

Fifty-one years later

44 was a first in the White House
Shattered the glass ceiling in politics
Some voters and some politicians reacted
With hatred, disrespect, and death threats
Boos and ridicule and calls for impeachment
Met 44 within his first 100 days

44 stayed focused signed a gender mender
Stopped the economic hemorrhaging, cleaned up
The war in Iraq/ratcheted down the other war
Signed healthcare legislation/brought the LBGTQ
Community out of the shadows/unrestricted women's
Access to the military, for him it's all been about fairness
Won healthcare for all against blockbuster ignorance

A small noisy knot of white obstructionists leading
Their lily-livered politicians in a hateful dive
Toward a great and monumental catastrophe refused
To surrender their loathing and it's become like
Leading a mad dog to sanity against its will as
These saboteurs stir a vengeful pot to a fury boil
A boil that will one day produce a despot

It will be written in history this truth of the progress
44 sought to bring about and this vindictive white
Fury blind that fought tooth and nail to hold on to
Their misconceptions it is in history that this truth
Will be written and after some time living with tyranny
All white Americans will finally come to cheer 44.

Last Words

My brother Ted lay on his back in his bed
His eyes light up when we enter the
Room, Gussie stays by the door
He greets me, Hey Horace, but his eyes
Speak already volumes — he is dying
I reach his bed lean over to kiss him
His mouth passes my face his lips making a
Sound that says he kissed me back

My already rehearsed comments fly away
The moment is so momentous, I love you, I say
His eyes say tell me something I don't already know
I recall the dozens of times we shopped together
And after shopping we walked to the same Irish pub
To eat pastrami, drink beer, and talk family
I remembered our adventures in a place we both
Loved dearly — Central Park
His eyes seem to be searching for matching recollections

There is so much more I want to recall with him
It would take a lifetime
The lifetime we had already spent
Plus he is tired

I will always treasure the times we had together
I say, you are the best brother I could have had
And I will forever carry you in my heart
I'm glad to hear that, he says, his eyes closed
And his mouth forms a satisfied configuration
Of triumph.

Haiku Ted

Ted's teeth were perfectly formed
And shown pearl white in his smile
Ted had a winning grin.

July 26, 2017

Today I found out that I am dying
(We are all dying from the day we are born, what I mean is:)
Today I was told that I have cancer
Non-small cell adenocarcinoma, the same monster
That took my father and younger brother
It has now shown up at my front door.

Life is suffering, so I acknowledge the cancer
I accept its presence
I concede its influence
I recognize its extremities, but
I shore up for the battle

We are going to occupy this same body
For some time my cancer and I

I'm surprised that I am able to face this fate and
All its dire possibilities without fear and panic
I even seem to be gaining a new focus
Of clarity an almost euphoric
So there you are — how do you do?

A new vista opens to a clearer view
Of my joys and my sorrows
While one sits with you in the twilight
The other awaits you at dusk
I become empty and balanced
Without joy nor sorrow
That is how I must remain

Have you come to answer the question
I have long held about death?
What's on the other side of this light of the world;
Will this time after life be like the eons before life?
Will I just return to where I once was —
I am eager for your answers though
I know what has to happen to experience
The secrets no mortal knows

My only resistance is I cling to my family
My wife, my sons, and my grandchildren
My mother, my aunts and my uncles, my sisters,
My nieces and my nephews
My cousins —

So I shore up for the battle to ease this sorrow on them

We are going to occupy this same body
For some time my cancer and I.

Death

Look through a window and you see outside
What is out there is revealed
Now look at the wall bordering either side
Of the window and all you see is the wall
The wonders out there are concealed —

Death is a window.

Bird Flying High

Charlie Parker's mother was a Choctaw Native
His father was a pianist, dancer, and singer
Bird's conception encompassed the ooze
Of that essence, he was what they brought
Him in the world to be
Black Choctaw Boy was Bird

He was there at the sound of the first trumpet
Dead bones arising, dead bones arising
A gift bestowed, it will take him far, but
The sacrifice is weighty and far-reaching
This price demanded of the artist by the
Creative energy using him for expression
Great God Almighty, dead bones arising
Bird flying high

The energy was in the spirit of the music
Articulated in blackness; live and energetic
The Spirit came to America in the sounds Africans
Bound and naked made on the slave ships
The Spirit was in the field hollers that replaced
The sounds of the slave ship's mayhem
The Spirit existed to shelter a whole people

The Spirit resides in the work songs of the first generation
The Spirit grew into the spirituals of the second generation
The Spirit infested the molecules of every black soul
In the shared experience of human degradation
The Spirit was in Kansas City to give Bird wings
That took Bird flying high in a bebop color spiral
Flying high was so alluring

America was still too dark a place to
Recognize the gift and the cost and
The consequences for high-flying Birds
So Bird found a way to fly fast and
Perilously low high flying

His sound lit the way it led
And sparked a movement
From New York to L.A.
The cats were digging his
Scrapple from the Apple

Although America set its limits Bird
Was able to break through to fly
Unrestricted, unreformed, trail blazing
Leaving tracks for those who followed

Black Choctaw Boy, flying high
Ooop Bop Sh' Bam; Hey Ba Ra Rebop
Black Choctaw Boy flying higher
Faster and perilously low to the ground

When the Devil strikes a covenant
The time to render comes sudden
Unannounced and irrevocable

Bird's infant daughter died and he
Hurried home and wandered off again
He could find no exit so he drank iodine
From the medicine cabinet
They pumped his stomach
Brought him back to life
But not to living
By now for Bird's flying high is a compulsion
And he goes back to the medicine cabinet
Ending up in a mental ward

High flying Bird is caged down to earth
Bird can't fly, Bird can't create
Bird can't Bird
A Saturday evening he wanders to the
Bebop Baroness Pannonica's fancy address
Killing time — she could see that he was ill and
Summoned her personal physician who
Wanted to hospitalize Bird, he refused
Dead bones arising, dead bones arising

And Sunday evening while sitting on
Her couch laughing and enjoying jugglers
On the *Ed Sullivan Show* Bird spread his
Wings to succumb to a pedestrian death
And flew away — Black Choctaw Boy.

The Strangest Fruit

Billie Holiday comes to the stage her
Voice laying bare her naked soul
Her eyes weary, her gardenia limp
From the toll America collects at
At every juncture of black life
Born to a teenage mother in the slums
Of Baltimore, Maryland, her way was
Troublesome, twice locked away at
The age of nine, sexually assaulted
The burdens of her life already forming
In her voice before she began to sing

She arose to the stage glowingly naked
The miseries of the world dripping from
Every syllable she uttered, our realities
Reverberating from her quivering voice
How long can her spirit endure it all?

She cast off her given name Eleanora Fagan
When her voice found her in Harlem speakeasies
To adopt a persona resilient enough to withstand
The black burdens of being a star with a second
Class status she toured with Artie Shaw's orchestra
Suffering the indignities of black American womanhood

Some of her plights were self-inflicted
Substance abuse, heavy drinking, boyfriends
And a long list of men who took advantage
Of her, her prestige, and her bank account
Oooh, What a Little Moonlight Can Do

Her song titles speak the truth of her life:
Lady Sings the Blues, God Bless the Child,
Good Morning Heartache, Don't Explain,
You Took Advantage of Me, My Man,
Billie's Blues, Body and Soul,
If the Moon Turns Green, Fine and Mellow,
The End of a Love Affair, Why Was I Born,
Riffin' the Scotch, Strange Fruit.

Billie Holiday lived the life she sang
About in her songs making her life an
Open book, her public witnessing
Every wound, every drink, every rage,
It's all there in the quiver of her voice.

Thelonious Sphere Monk

I was floored when Charlie Ricco
Brought him to my room (in my mother's house)
I played a recording he made with
The "Trane"
He pranced to the beat
And recreated his riff
Only one of five jazzmen
To grace the cover of *Time*
Magazine pioneer in bebop
We spoke then they left

I was just out of the Army
Making a hustle until I found
Work

Monk was exceptional in many things
Math, physics, and ping-pong and
It's cool that he referred to himself as
The-onlyest Monk

Monk rose from Minton's Playhouse
'Round Midnight
Using silence and hesitation
In a style never heard before
Made them go Straight No Chaser
I remembered our conversation
Then
In Walked Bud.

Art as a Way of Life

(For Hampton Olfus)

This artist is tall with long lean delicate fingers
His hair is in the form of the original man
His skin is clear and his gut is stiff from
Healthy and meticulous consumption

He connects his art to the eternal
To express the truth he finds
In this world and this life

His paintings are layered with eyes
Where there are no seers
Visions where there are no visionaries
Thoughts where there are no thinkers
Love where there are no lovers

This artist creates the world
As it can one day be
His art is a way of life.

Old Hambone

Old Hambone had many dreams
Visions of grand splendors
In one he imagined words
With unblemished illuminations
Attached in a lineage to truth
And he sat with crossed-leg satisfaction

Old Hambone had many dreams
Revelations of universal majesty
In one the prophecy of human
Deliverance lay fulfilled
And God's smile glistened
And he chanted his gratification

Old Hambone had many dreams
Interpretations of inspiring sounds
He heard the call in Gabriel's horn
When the bebop players revealed
Resonances of racial inequality
And he bopped to the beat of clarity
That sustained black people's faith

Old Hambone had another dream
A mirage of enamored duality
Stirred by an innocent temptress
Whose intentions proved her virtue
In this case she pleaded not guilty
And Old Hambone agreed
It all just ain't meant to be.

The Ocean

There must be some murky
Cosmic truth in the rhythm
Of the waves upon the shore

What are the secrets infused
In the white frosty clusters
That ride the crest of the waves
Perpetually
Rise and fall in an illusion
Come then gone in a
Never-ending replication?

The Living Earth

Two places where you can notice
The curvature of the earth are at
The beach and up in an airplane

To get the sensation of earth's
Majestic massiveness
Let your eyes gaze upon the curving
Horizon at the beach — draw an
Imaginary line from as far as
You can see on your left and
On your right back to where you lie
Like a giant pizza slice then
Estimate how many more slices
You would have to make to complete
The pie — there before you — the enormity
Of the earth

While you're in this state of being
Lying before the horizon on the beach
Search within your own body
For a feel of the earth's motion
As it revolves and as it also propels
Around the sun and you know that
Earth is alive with a resonant mission.

Awaken to the Dream

I arrived to this consciousness
Screaming from the sudden
Jolt of awareness

The journey from naught
To wakefulness is startling
To scream is my only impulse

It is a scream absent judgment
Not of joy nor sorrow
It is a primordial sound

Realities gather and assemble
And form for me an identity
And I have experiences which
Solidified my identity and
Give me preference and other
Impulses; desires, urges, instincts
And whims

I am not alone, this perception
Of consciousness is widely shared
We are a community encountering
The same fantasy, the same delusion
The same hallucination

We name everything; we call it
The cosmos, the galaxies, the solar system
The sun, the moon, the stars
The world, our world — earth

We divide the darkness from
The light and name them Day
And Night and count the days and nights
It takes our earth to travel around the sun
We call it a year, we count the ticks
And the tocks between the occurrence
Of Day and Night and divide them into
Hours, minutes, and seconds

We create time
The creation of time necessitates
The need to record what happens
During the tally of time — history
We are a community encountering
The same fantasy, the same delusion
The same hallucination, but our impulses,
Desires, urges, instincts, and whims differ
Altering our realities and tolerance
A division that creates abrasions
And disunity, and conflicts and
Clans and tribes and countries and
Wars, and deaths and sufferings
And a reality no longer propelled
By the same perceptions

A routine is established
Monotony sets in to collect —
Consciousness dulls, controls
Are lost — some move ahead
A hierarchy emerges
Serfdom begins
Awareness is manipulated

Time flees

You are
Where you are

Things are
What they are

The reality
Is real
You think

Everything has a place
Order is time-honored

Disruptions and peace
Alternate in existence

To maintain the central objective
Ascension to the top of the pyramid

The divisions become many
Natural, synthetic, imagined
Geographical, cultural

Race and ethnicity stand
A major barrier

The more I look at a thing
The clearer it becomes to me
That I don't see a thing — elusive

My search is on to make sense
Of my perceptions — why am I here?
Why are we here and can't we all just
Get along?

We are all overwhelmed by
The rapid occurrence of
Change while too many
Things stay the same

I move to disengage from
The sense of community
I need to save myself from
The perceptions
We are all locked into

One day I bumped into the Tao
And read: to empty myself
Of all feelings, become without thought
Emotionless, opinionless, desireless
Detached and vacant, like dead wood

It was long and hard and often failing
To purge the years of habit and ritual
It took a concentrated practice, but
Finally I arrived, a hollowed vessel
Ready to awaken to the dream of
Reality, now I'm able to disrobe from
The notion of birth and death
To return to my natural self

Like A Zulu Prince

He was born an Englishman in Hackney, London
In his room he learned to play a given guitar gift
Left school at sixteen to pursue a musical career
Made it to the top of the hard rock, heavy metal
Music genre, guitarist, vocalist, songwriter, achiever

Honed an image as a shirtless idol with Def Leppard
And even before his friend died of too much alcohol
He abandoned smoke, meat, and alcohol, replaced them
With an Eastern religion, martial arts and kickboxing

Life in Orange County turned him into a Californian in
Ways other than location — three times altar married mostly
To Zulu chicks, with the blackest beauty on the side, Zulu
Chicks became his thing, black girls who regarded their blackness
In a way that his whiteness was needed to ease their pain
Zulu chicks who birthed his fair-skinned broods far and wide

As his geographical harem spread, he longed to gather
His concubines and his progenies all in, if not one
Combine, at least in one state — California — where this
Lily-white Englishman could recline under the tropical
Evergreens, the mahogany and the ebony trees
Eating kola nuts, and rubbing palm oil, his concubines
Providing a cool breeze with palm fans and he living
Life like a Zulu prince of old.

Life Partners

(for Gussie)

I was once young and looking for you
You were once young and looking too
We were both once young our hearts apart

The universe is wonder and mystery
The ordained is the ordained or did we
Meet through the quirk of possibilities
On this most horrible day for the nation
And a most wonderful day for us we will
Always remember November 22, 1963

The universe conspired to have us meet
Planned or quirk — it happened and
We took control from there to
Form this lasting bond of 55 years

The years have flown by with laughter and tears
All a confirmation to our commitment to this union
We raised our sons to families of their own

And now in these golden years we smile
A knowing smile of assurance
For the love we shared for all these years.

A Southern Black Girl of the 1930s

(for Aunt Ruth)

Born with ambition in a land where
She was discriminated against because
She was female, Southern, uneducated
And black, she learned that to fulfill her
Dreams she had to leave the South

She had a married cousin in Harlem
In New York City where she joined
Them after living alone in rooming houses
With tree-lined streets and landlords
Who were saberless pirates plundering
All who came North to escape racial evil

She landed a manufacturing job in the
Garment center and joined a union
She worked hard and opened a bank
Account and paid faithfully her union
Dues — she loved the union — and believed
That the union secured her future

And when her sister with three children
In the South had troubles and needed to
Escape the South and an abusive husband
She paved the way, first brought up the older
Boy, then finding a larger apartment to suit
Her cousin and her husband and her sister and
The other two children making a freedom run

Being unable to have children of her own
She guided her sister's family's transition to
Public housing and independence and
Oversaw her sister's family's improvement

She developed an interest in attaining
The education she didn't receive in the South
And enrolled in an adult continuing education
Program paid for by the union

She met a man; an ambitious West Indian
They married and their bank accounts became
Like their children; they nourished them and
They grew, both having been born in the Depression
They lived a Spartan existence in public housing
She haggled like the people she saw getting
Ahead in 1940s New York City

Her strong desire for motherhood
Led them to adopt a baby girl and
They nourished her like their bank
Account and she grew and did well
In church and school and life was
Now like the American dream

When their daughter went off
To college, the husband forgot
His wife's name, then he forgot
His name and he forgot other things
How to care for himself, how to put
A fork to his mouth, he was retirement age
And so was she; she spent her days
Caring for him in all ways — and her nights too

He died in their bed
It went to her head
She was alone, but he left her well
And still she haggled like the people
Who got ahead; a 97-year-old
Well-to-do widow with the financial
Attitude of a Depression-era pauper

She was cared for and looked after
By her niece, her sister's child who
She helped raised and now she loved
God even more than she ever loved
Her union and trusted that God would
See her through to the end, she often
Said of future events — If God Say So.

A Southern Black Girl

(for Mag)

My mother married young to a soldier
From the Red Ball Express when she
Was not yet 21 and he 24 and I near 4
She fled a few years later from his brutality
Instigated by the inequality of the South
Which kept access to GI benefits from him
And his kind to guide them back into the
Serfdom of their prewar days to drive out
Any retention of the manhood grown on
The fields of battle in Europe so he
Struck out at those closest to him

In a bustling Harlem in New York City
In 1946 with three children and a thin
Support net of a single loving sister and
The welfare system of a then generous
City, my mother, a young uneducated
Black Southern girl braved the odds
In a city of six million strangers

She was lucky to get public housing
In a safe section of the city and there
She raised her three children, soon to be four
Without major big-city incidents: no drugs
No juvenile delinquency, no jail
The youngest boy and the youngest girl
Graduated college

She spoke to everyone unfiltered
Often sounding harsh, crude, even
Abrasive, but neighbors flocked to her
A wide network of friends who cared
They loved the authenticity of this simple
Country girl alone in the darkened world
Making a way for her children

She worked in the hotel industry
And retired with a tiny pension
One of her friends introduced her
To Jehovah the Witness and helped
Her to study to become a disciple
Through her devotion she grew
In faith and understanding
To overcome many adversities

As of now, she lived for 70 years
In that same apartment she raised
Her children since 1950 and returns
South once in a while to visit her
94-year-old brother and her oldest son
Who returned to the soil middle aged

In 2019 she turned 97 years old and
She is on her third or fourth harvest
Of friends because she outlived them all
While sailing forward with the motto
Ninety-nine and a half won't do.

Barbara

My youngest sister was born
When I was already a teenager
So I minded her by rocking her
Singing to silence her crying

We sat on the sofa, my younger
Brother and sister to pass Barbara
Around as we sing to quiet her
Discomfort with family love

That she sprang from a different
Well was never born to discord
We were all from one mother
And that is the tie that binds us

There are times when I can see
The chasm in our difference but
There has never been a time when
These differences interfered much
With the love that connects us all.

Helen Deas, Caregiver

She rolled into the role slowly
And without planned intentions
Picked up a prescription here
Called for a doctor's appointment
Learned the rules of a health insurance
Policy and the language spoken in
Doctor's offices and how to speak
To the medical field with language
That placed her on equal footing

As our mother and aunt grew in age
Helen applied what she had acquired
In knowledge of the medical labyrinth
On their behalf, all the while she still
Held down the demands of a stressful
Job and as they grew older their medical
Conditions worsened and required
Helen to know more; about recognizing
Certain medical symptoms; assessing
The proficiency of doctors and staff
Researching medicines and identifying
Detrimental side effects and even at
Times, overriding the decisions of doctors

Their health care her main charge
And concern, but there are personal
Practical, social, and familial matters
As well, shopping, bills, transportation
Spiritual, amusements — all to attend
To to make living and life complete

Helen dove into her chores of making
Life livable for two very senior Southern
Born ladies as if it were her vocation and
Indeed it became so; she nursed them
Through their 70s and their 80s and now
Halfway through their 90s and one still going
Wobbly at times, but still moving ahead
To reach that century mark.

Poem for My Father

I like to think that I turned out to
Be the person my father would
Have wanted himself to be

He grew up in a largely different
America — an America of denials
Of basic services and opportunities

A Southern boy at a time when
Little or no money was allotted
To educate descendants of slaves

He achieved in that one-room school
House the rudiments of reading and
Writing and how to count in their heads

He grew into the skill of deception
Letting smiles hide his scorn, it was
A trait passed down from generations

The damage this ruse caused to
His psyche hid its incremental
Impairment in self-destructiveness

The violence and the drunkenness
The rowdiness and misconduct are
Seen as a normal fact of Negro life

The time arose when the government
Needed his body, trained him for war
And to drive big-wheel military trucks

A member of the Red Ball Express
He performed a vital service that
Helped to win the war against fascism

Without ceremony, appreciation, or
Reward they returned him to his
Prior condition in the racist South

That South that concealed from him
The benefits of the GI Bill which
Would have improved his standing

Afford him housing and education, allow him to
Avert some of the pitfalls of racism in his character
His life, his family, his marriage, his future

The South heaved him back to the black abyss
Unwittingly he fell back into old cruel habits
Of oblivious drunken mindlessness and violence

That broke his family apart and separated him
From his wife and children who fled not just
Him, but the South as well, in a run for freedom

Now alone and unattached he roamed the
Countryside living the carefree days and the
Oblivious nights in a hazardous recklessness

Midlife caught up to him to settle him
Down before the family's cancer gene
Struck to bring him to a life of reflection

On the other hand I came about in an
America struggling to shed the reminiscence
Of its original sin creating a tiny space for me

I went to college on the GI Bill, found
And worked a job that allowed me to
Raise a family and love my wife

I even had the luxury of a profession
Possible only when one's not burdened
By the drudgery of a substandard life

From his time to mine, the needle moved
Nine, to my breed America's not been kind
My generation's put it all on the line

Still I like to think that I turned
Out to be the person my father
Would have wanted himself to be.

Bogging with Mama Dolly

When summer came I went south
To Mama Dolly's house in
Hollywood, South Carolina
This house where I was born
And spent my first three years

Mama Dolly was always happy
To have me there to pass on
Traditions and insights too and
To feed me huckleberry dumplings
Berries picked from the huckleberry patch

But what I liked best were the days
She gathered up a croaker sack and
Clawed sticks and kept track of the
Time for low tide and she knew
What time to set out to the creek
To finish our walk at low tide's peak

Bare feet we walked on the hot earth
Till we reached the mud-marsh of
The creek and I followed in her tracks
As she instructed so I would be safe
From making a perilous bogging step

The crabs were hidden under mud
Anxious of our presence only an
Air bubble betrayed their positions
We pressed our sticks down until
We felt their backs and reached our
Hands down into the mud to grab
Them safely from behind their claws

Washed the mud from them with
Water from the shallow stream
And put them into the croaker sack
That rested on Mama Dolly's sturdy back

And when we had more than merely
A snack in the sack she put moss on
The crabs in the croaker sack as we
Walked back, of this I never asked why
A mystery remains whose answer I lack

This was typical of my summer stay with my
Grandmother, my teacher, my moral guide
My controlling light, my troubadour, my love
And the week before school began again in
New York City I packed my bags for the
Train ride that took me away from my bliss.

ON HUMAN RIGHTS

American politicians, the American media
And that freed privileged segment of the
American people always want American
Leaders and diplomats to press the other
Countries of the world about their human
Rights record; their treatments of their citizens
America lectures:

Don't slaughter them in Cambodia
Don't imprison them in Russia
Don't starve them in North Korea
Don't poison gas them in Syria
Don't famine them in Mali
Doesn't force marry them in Saudi Arabia
Doesn't suicide bomb them in Iraq
Don't create refugees of them in Somalia

America will travel the world pointing
A finger of superiority at these human rights
Violations in other countries while it turns a
Blind eye to the plight of black and brown
People within its own borders where these
Don'ts also apply

Don't prison pipeline them around the country
Doesn't poison water them in Flint
Don't disenfranchise them in the South
Don't execute them unarmed around the country
Don't redline them around the country
Don't miseducate them around the country
Don't restrict medical care from them around the country
Don't gentrify them in the cities

America must turn its attention inward
To learn that its human rights record is
Dismal from its very creation
And the other countries of the world owe
It to America to tell it so
My God, America, have you no shame?

These Times

These are troubling days
And nights too
To watch the seams of America's
Carefully stitched-together laws
Bludgeoned open by a reckless
Dangling marionette controlled
By greed and unseen hands

A wicked puppet with a spell
Deep and unbreakable
Cast over parts of the land
A brightly tinted logo
Offering bleak outcomes
Dressed like populace drippings

He is often like an octopus
With twenty tentacles all
Stretching out in multiple
Directions all at once breaching
The seams of democracy

The response is probingly methodic
Strictly orthodox legitimacy that
Lags behind in time
So that it is down here when
The tentacle is up there

Of the outcome no one knows
Whether good can come from
Behind to overcome evil.

The Sea Island Mungins

"The finest picture of the Sea Island Negroes ever written; Simple, vivid, and taut ... raw and outspoken," reads the *Library Journal*'s back cover blurb for the novel *Here Come Joe Mungin*, written by Chalmers S. Murray. The novel was published by G.P. Putnam's Sons in 1942 and reissued by Bantam Books in 1954. I am a descendant of those Sea Island Mungins. In 1999, when I became aware of Murray's novel making our name a part of the folk history of the South, a natural curiosity welled up in me to find out more about Murray — and more about the Mungin people and our name.

Murray, a white native of Edisto Island, South Carolina, was born in 1894 and grew up amongst the descendants of the slaves of the Sea Islands, so he knew them well — so well, in fact, that his parents carefully "screened" the black boys he played with. His father made $2,000 a year operating a general merchandise store "that catered largely to the Negroes," Murray recalls in *Turn Backward O Time in Your Flight*, his 1960 reminiscence of growing up on Edisto Island.

The North and South Edisto Rivers separate Edisto Island from the mainland of South Carolina. The 55-square-mile island is one of the oldest settlements in the state. This is also the island where General Sherman left 10,000 sick and starving freedmen who had joined him on his march to Georgia, because he was unable to provide for them.

Murray and his sister grew up on their father's farm in an area populated by blacks and isolated from the other white people on the island. The boy found his sister and a female cousin, who visited sometimes, unsuitable as playmates. "My parents did, however, approve of the children of a Negro family nearby, the Baileys. They were respectable people, my father said, and when time came for me to attend school, he hired Joseph Bailey (who was a few years older than I) as a yard boy."

One of the yard boy's duties was to drive his young white charge to school in the Murray family's buggy hauled by their mare Nellie. The two boys became constant companions, Murray recollects without any recognition of the following irony: "My mother thought so highly of him that she gave him lessons in the afternoon, since his job prevented him from attending school." This was during the first years of the twentieth century when, in South Carolina, the black children went to school six months of the year and the white students attended school for nine months of the year. "The whites thought this was fair enough. In fact, many of them did not approve of spending tax money to support Negro schools. They seem to think that the State Legislature was over-generous in giving the Negro children any kind of an education."

The Murray family lived well from the money that came in from the general merchandise store and from the farm. They weren't rich, not even well off, but the dire economic condition of the area's Negro population made it possible for the family to have a servant for every chore. A woman named Maum Rachel cleaned the Murray home, tended to their chickens, and cared for their vegetable garden. She was also the cook and part-time nurse, all for a well spent five dollars a month. Another servant did the laundry. The yard boy cared for the horses. The black foreman, Joe Middleton, who was the model for Murray's protagonist in the novel, was so highly thought of that he was paid a dollar a day while the other male field hands received fifty cents, and the women earned thirty cents a day. "My mother never called the place a farm however. Though the acreage was small, she referred to it as a 'plantation.'"

Murray gained his knowledge of the Negro people in his region by being raised among them. He also had an opportunity to further his study from his work as a writer on the Federal Writers' Project (FWP) documenting the work and history of the Works Progress Administration (WPA) road projects in South Carolina where blacks and whites found work during the Depression. Murray's experience working for the WPA, where he wrote several essays on the racial composition and conditions of work crews in his area of South Carolina, would later be useful to him. The FWP had an office in every state and hired 6,000 people from 1935 until 1942; its mission was to document the entire American culture and landscape. As it turned out, the FWP was more than mere temporary employment for Depression-era writers; it stimulated the careers of many talented writers. Murray was in the distinguished company of Richard Wright, Margaret Walker, Zora Neale Hurston, Studs Terkel, and Saul Bellow, to name a few.

Murray grew up around Negro spirituals and superstitions, he stored knowledge of Negro myths and folk sayings, he understood the area's Gullah speech, and in his writings often seems charmed by them. He knew the rituals of the Negro churches and the difference in sophistication the black preachers from Charleston had over the rural island black preachers. During his work with the FWP he learned Negro work songs, saw what they ate, witnessed their despair, observed their rage, and gained a gauge for their temperaments. He was well-suited to write *Here Come Joe Mungin*, his "… raw and outspoken" novel of the Sea Island Negroes.

Murray attended the Citadel Military Academy in Charleston, but was ostracized by his fellow cadets for reporting the names of the upperclassmen who hazed him. He was picked on and singled out for demerits. Murray describes his time at the Citadel as like being in "purgatory." Then came the First World War and Murray jumped at the chance to leave the Citadel. His application for an officer's commission was, he believed, purposely mishandled. To avoid serving as a draftee he volunteered for the Army and because of his prior training at the Citadel was appointed to the rank of sergeant in a few weeks.

After the war, Murray returned to Edisto Island, where he married Faith Cornish and began his writing career. They had two daughters, Faith and Jane. In a recent interview, Jane Murray McCollum, a retired librarian who lived with her husband in Greenville, South Carolina, remembered her father as a particular man who favored punctuality. They often took a rowboat to the ferry that took them to the mainland, and Murray always fussed with his family to be on time. "He typed with two fingers and wouldn't stand for us to make any noises while he was working," she recalls. Murray had published two novels before he wrote *Here Come Joe Mungin*, and the knowledge he gained, both in terms of craft and subject matter during his days with the FWP, would now come to fruition.

When people asked me about the origin of my unusual name, I told them a story I made up about the early Mungins hiding out on the Sea Islands to avoid slavery. They were discovered in the 1880s and told that slavery was over, thus we came through the period with our original African name intact. I attribute our name to Africa because of Njoroge Mungai (pronounced Moong-gi), the Kenyan medical doctor who became Kenya's foreign affairs minister in 1969. I think that Mungin (often mispronounced Moong-gi) may be an Americanization of Mungai because I have never known a white Mungin. Many African Americans received their surnames from their slave owners. My ancestors without a doubt were slaves, but what explains how we maintained our identity? Where are the white Mungins of the Sea Islands?

I own a book published by Halbert's Family Heritage that lists all the Mungins they could find in public records in Europe, North America, and South Africa. In the United States, Sea Island Mungins are concentrated in South Carolina, Georgia, and Florida, with smaller numbers in New York, California and Washington State. There are also populations of Mungins large enough to mention in Great Britain, Germany, and Canada. Of the six hundred towns with the largest population of Mungin households in South Carolina, Hollywood (72), in Charleston County, has the most, and it is the town of my birth.

It might have been the publisher's Eurocentric bearing or a realization that it would be a nearly impossible undertaking to hunt public records, say a telephone directory, in the underdeveloped nations on Africa's West Coast, which caused this listing to be incomplete. That there were no searches in Senegal, Sierra Leone, Ivory Coast, and Ghana — where most African slaves came from — cuts both ways. It may be that there are no Mungins in these countries, but until there are attempts to research the name in these places and the questions are answered one way or the other, my suspicion remains intact.

My nephew Lateef Mungin, who was an investigative reporter with the *Atlanta Journal Constitution*, applied his investigative skills to solving this mystery. He traveled to the Sea Islands, where he found out that there is a river in the Daufuskie area named the Mungin River; further research revealed that there was once an Irishman in the area who owned slaves — slaves who carried his name as was the tradition elsewhere in the South. Today, I am Facebook friends with a white Mungin from Ireland, so while the mystery of the Mungin name is settled, the mystique lives on.

The main character in Murray's novel is forged from the life of Joe Middleton, who the Murrays adored, and young Murray idolized. Middleton was an atheist, a celebrated married ladies' man, and foreman at the Murray farm. "Joe was a tall lanky man, and he had no beauty. He loved to fight and to drink, but he never got drunk. He was afraid of nobody and would tackle two or three men at a time, if his opponents made him angry enough. He liked nothing so much as a sharp argument and would out-talk anyone in the neighborhood," which are many of the traits that defined the Mungins from that period and beyond.

During this period, there were also Mungins quietly getting an education at the Penn School, a privately funded institution established on nearly all-black St. Helena Island, prior to the Civil War, to educate Negroes. It is conceivable that Murray used Mungin for his title character because the name was widely known. Murray found the name's association with the rowdy nature of rural Negroes, at the bottom of society in the post-reconstructed South, appropriate for the tone of his novel. The Mungin name lent authenticity to his main character's raging ambition to eat and, perhaps, even to prosper, at any cost.

The novel begins on St. Helena Island with the murder of August Mungin on the same day his third child was born. Joe Lincoln Mungin was named after the biblical Joseph and the emancipator Abraham Lincoln. His uncle, Rufus Mungin, named him the day after avenging the baby's father's murder. After he buried his brother, Rufus was in a pious mood that induced a vision of the baby's future greatness. These two names, Rufus felt, would ensure that Joe Lincoln Mungin would be a conqueror.

And it was a good thing that Rufus acted with dispatch in naming the baby, for in the next two pages, which covered a time period of six years, he too was killed. Rufus had been visiting the wife of a much younger man. When the husband became aware of Rufus's transgressions, he had his sorceress grandmother put a hex on him. Six years old and curious, young Joe had gone down to the creek looking for the ocean when he happened upon the young man and the sorceress talking up the spell that would kill Rufus. The boy ran back to tell his mother what he had heard so she could warn Rufus, but when he arrived home they were already mourning his death.

At the age of seventeen, Joe set out from St. Helena Island determined to claw his way to the top of the bottom in this life. He was tall, gangly,s and strong. He took the boat to Etiwan Island, where he would live with his mother's bother, Uncle Isaac Durrell. There were many plantations, lots of work, and a chance to rise on Etiwan Island. All Joe had was the clothes on his back and a scrawny live hen his mother gave him as a parting gift. Joe made his first conquest minutes into the trip. A boat hand offered him fifteen cents for the hen. Joe sold him the hen for a dollar after convincing him that the chicken was raised by a witchcraft woman and could be used to make spells that would win him the favors of women. Joe was determined to give up his inexperienced country-boy ways and finagle his way to the top.

The author's familiarity with the sights and sounds, the plants, and the smells of the creeks of the Sea Islands are transferred to his characters. He understands and shares the Sea Island Negro's love of oysters, mullet, and yellow yams, and, he loves to portray the men's affection for fat, sassy women. Murray describes them in a variety of sexual deviations including pedophilia. He glorifies the perpetual fighting. He seems sympathetic to the harshness of their existence, jealous of their constant drinking, and envious of their womanizing.

Isaac met Joe when the boat arrived at the Etiwan landing. On the walk to Isaac's house, they came upon a group of girls playing in the woods. Among them was Tyra Ann Wright. She was only thirteen, but had the shape of a woman. Joe was mesmerized with the girls' play and by Tyra Ann's comely body. He lagged behind his disapproving uncle and in a conversation he had with Tyra Ann, he promised her three gunger cakes if she would meet him by the general store at dusk. When Joe caught up to his uncle, he was warned about Tyra Ann and her family — the Wrights, whom Isaac described as a wicked breed.

After his uncle introduced him to Mr. Hamilton, the plantation owner, and he was assigned his work chores, Joe returned to his uncle's shack for a short while before he set out for his rendezvous with Tyra Ann. He had the gunger cakes, wrapped in old newspaper, ready when Tyra arrived at the general store. He gave her the cakes and they walked off into the woods. Joe's heart was thumping as he heard Tyra Ann's footsteps behind him. When they were a quarter-mile from any houses, Tyra Ann directed Joe down into a gully, muddy from recent showers. He heard rustling in the leaves and whispered words. He stopped to listen. Four of Tyra Ann's playmates hid in the bushes. Suddenly from the still came a wad of red mud that landed on Joe's face. Then another in his mouth and he was pelted over and over with wet red mud. The boy looked around, puzzled and full of rage, and then he realized Tyra Ann was nowhere in sight. Joe could hear his female tormentors in the distance laughing and calling out his name, "Here come Joe Mungin." He had no idea that six years from then Tyra Ann Wright would become his wife.

During the next years, Joe worked hard attending to the plantation cows and trying to get promoted to plowman, but things seldom went right. He drank a lot, got into too many fights, and finally got fired for trying to force himself on a young girl. His uncle knew the owner of another plantation on the other side of the island and recommended Joe for a job there. On his way to the new plantation, Joe went through a retrospection of his behavior and became newly committed to getting ahead. He was now determined to make the attempt to get along with people. He would never back down from a fight, but he wouldn't initiate one either. He would use his ability to be glib or sliver-tongued, as it was known, to triumph over his rivals and enemies. His goals were to save enough to buy some land and plant his own crops and build himself a home and have a family.

William Morton was the owner of the Jack Daw Hall Plantation. His main crops were cotton and corn. The Negro families worked as independent contractors, and were assigned acreage to farm and a shack to live in. Although Morton treated everyone humanely and fair, to be assigned prime acreage created fierce competition amongst the families. Joe got a feel for every nuance of the place right away. He worked hard and impressed Morton and his fellow workers as a man who was striving to prosper. In a few years, he had risen from yard boy to plowman and had an eleven acre plot to plant.

Shortly after Joe had made his mark and was a leader and most prominent of the plantation's workers, the entire Wright family migrated to the Jack Daw Hall Plantation. Joe met Tyra Ann again and that very day they decided to marry. The Wright family approved of her marriage to this man, who, it was widely believed, would someday be the foreman. With Tyra Ann married to the plantation foreman, the Wright family schemed, they would be in position to work only prime land.

The marriage between Joe and Tyra Ann didn't go well for long. She plotted against him from the beginning. She didn't want to share his accomplishments; she wanted to shape and control them. When it became clear that Tyra Ann was barren, she took in two of her sister's children to help in the fields and around the house. Joe took up with a flock of outside women and, as some men do, he rationalized that he was determined not to waste his seed. Soon there was a small army of Jo's "bush chillun" spread out around the plantation. Then the day arrived — the old foreman became gravely ill and could work no longer. Joe became the new foreman — big boss man — with a wife, a half dozen outside women, and a gaggle of children.

Joe was eventually able to buy some land for himself, which he worked during his time off from his plantation job. He bought parcels of land and put them in the names of each outside woman, so that they and the children he fathered with them could make the land productive and profitable for themselves and for him. Then he bought a few cows, some pigs, and even a horse, and rode in a buggy like a white man. Joe had prospered, but his marriage was a nightmare. Tyra Ann schemed with her family against her husband and plotted in a failed attempt with a witch doctor woman to put her spell on him. Tyra Ann's knowledge of the outside women and children didn't bother

her much. Her frustration was that she had not yet conquered Joe. He beat her regularly, drank his liquor, arranged his nights around his outside women, and outfoxed her at every turn.

One day, on a visit to another part of the island, Tyra Ann met an old witch doctor man named Andrew Barron and his wife, Hester, a much younger woman. They were from St. Helena Island. Tyra Ann spoke with Barron privately and tried to get him to work a spell for her without telling him on whom she wanted the spell worked. He refused, explaining that he was a God-fearing man and that he only used his powers whenever his, or God's, wrath had been aroused by evil. When Tyra Ann returned home, she suggested that her husband hire two new hands for the plantation. She told him about the old man and his wife and she mentioned that they were both from St. Helena Island. Hester was a good-looking woman, but Tyra Ann didn't feel she needed to declare that. Tyra Ann knew that if the two came to Jack Daw Hall Plantation, Joe could not resist having Hester, and what woman could resist the call of Joe — the big boss-man. Maybe then witch doctor Andrew Barron's wrath would be awakened and her dearest dream would come true.

Indeed, the plantation foreman was interested in new workers and rode out to where the Barrons lived to offer them living quarters and field work. Barron spoke about people on St. Helena he thought Joe might know, but Joe just nodded. He couldn't keep his eyes away from Hester. Barron thanked Joe for the opportunity and, in a few days, they arrived at the plantation. In three months, what went on between Joe and Hester was widely known by their spouses and everyone else. Tyra Ann beseeched the witch doctor to put an end to the deceit and betrayal they both suffered.

He agreed to pray on it.

The next morning, Joe awoke in a heavy sweat, his heart thumped, and he found it hard to swallow. Before he made any attempt to get out of bed, he received a visitor. It was Andrew Barron inquiring whether Joe had misery in his head yet. Then it came to Joe that he knew this man from back home on St. Helena Island. It wasn't Barron's face that he felt acquainted with, but rather, his voice. As Barron stood above Joe haranguing him for sinning with Hester, Joe's mind went back to when he was a little boy searching for the ocean and he happened upon the young man and the sorceress calling up a spell on his Uncle Rufus. Barron's face was now old and wrinkled, but Joe was certain that this was the same voice he heard all those many years ago — and now he also knew that he was going to die.

Joe died, but his bush children went on, one supposes, as did the real life Mungins, to "rise in this life." Today, the achievements of the extended Sea Island Mungins family range from a death-row poet with a website to a Harvard-educated lawyer who has written a book about his experience with corporate racism. In between, there are lawyers, preachers, print and radio reporters, professional sports figures, doctors, writers, policemen, a union official, a communication director with high governmental security clearance, a community leader with an educational institution named after him, entrepreneurs, and soldiers — lots of soldiers.

Many Mungin men and lately, women, have used the military as a means to better themselves. Service records show that three Mungins received pensions for serving during the Civil War. Draft registration cards show that five Mungins were drafted for World War I and II, but I suspect more than five served in World War II. There are Mungins still alive today who served in the Korean conflict. There was one Mungin death in Vietnam, but scores of Mungins served — three brothers from one family alone. There were Mungins in Bosnia and there are Mungins serving in the U.S. Armed Forces around the world today. The Sea Island Mungins have served their nation well.

There are still many Mungins who have not obtained the American dream, but the story of the Sea Island Mungins is the American story of hope, perseverance, and achievement. Chalmers S. Murray took note of this fact more than half a century ago.

CPSIA information can be obtained
at www.ICGtesting.com
Printed in the USA
FSHW012106090521
81231FS

9 781929 647514